ROADMAP *to* Success

KEN BLANCHARD

STEPHEN COVEY

JEFF WOLF

Insight Publishing

Interior formatting and design: Brittany Stewart
Cover graphic design: Emmy Shubert
Editor: Sandra Pinkoski

10 9 8 7 6 5 4 3 2

Printed in the United States by
Insight Publishing Company
647 Wall Street
Sevierville, Tennessee 37862

ISBN   978-1-60013-250-6

Table of Contents

A Message from the Publisher

I've done a lot of driving in my life and one thing I have been smart enough to have is a dependable roadmap. If you don't have a good plan to get from where you are to where you want to go, you will get lost.

I've known many people who have started out in business and thought they had a good plan, but did not achieve the success they wanted. A major problem for many of these people was that they had not sought good advice from people who had achieved success. If you don't learn from the experience of others, you might achieve success but you will probably get there the hard way. You might get lost down many side roads before you find the right one.

Roadmap to Success is a mini-seminar on how to plan for your success. The successful people in this book have the experience that will help you find what you need to create your roadmap to success. These perceptive businesspeople were fascinating as they unfolded their own personal roadmaps and told me about their various success journeys.

I invite you to set aside some quiet time and learn from these exceptional authors. I assure you that your time won't be wasted. It's not often that you can access such a large quantity of quality information that will either get you started or help you get further along on your road to success. This book is an investment in your future—your successful future!

Interviews Conducted by:
David E. Wright, President
International Speakers Network &
Insight Publishing

An Interview with…

Dr. Stephen Covey

Chapter One

An interview with…

Dr. Stephen Covey

David E. Wright (Wright)

We're talking today with Dr. Stephen R. Covey, cofounder and vice-chairman of Franklin Covey Company, the largest management company and leadership development organization in the world. Dr. Covey is perhaps best known as author of *The 7 Habits of Highly Effective People,* which is ranked as a number one best-seller by the *New York Times,* having sold more than fourteen million copies in thirty-eight languages throughout the world. Dr. Covey is an internationally respected leadership authority, family expert, teacher, and organizational consultant. He has made teaching principle-centered living and principle-centered leadership his life's work. Dr. Covey is the recipient of the Thomas More College Medallion for Continuing Service to Humanity and has been awarded four honorary doctorate degrees. Other awards given Dr. Covey include the Sikh's 1989 International Man of Peace award, the 1994 International Entrepreneur of the Year award, *Inc.* magazine's Services Entrepreneur of the Year award, and in 1996 the National Entrepreneur of the Year Lifetime Achievement award for Entrepreneurial leadership. He has also been recognized as one of *Time* magazine's twenty-five most influential

Americans and one of *Sales and Marketing Management's* top twenty-five power brokers. As the father of nine and grandfather of forty-four, Dr. Covey received the 2003 National Fatherhood Award, which he says is the most meaningful award he has ever received. Dr. Covey earned his undergraduate degree from the University of Utah, his MBA from Harvard, and completed his doctorate at Brigham Young University. While at Brigham Young he served as assistant to the President and was also a professor of Business Management and Organizational Behavior.

Dr. Covey, welcome to *Roadmap to Success*.

Dr. Stephen Covey (Covey)

Thank you.

Wright

Dr. Covey, most companies make decisions and filter them down through their organization. You, however, state that no company can succeed until individuals within it succeed. Are the goals of the company the result of the combined goals of the individuals?

Covey

Absolutely—if people aren't on the same page, they're going to be pulling in different directions. To teach this concept, I frequently ask large audiences to close their eyes and point north, and then to keep pointing and open their eyes. They find themselves pointing all over the place. I say to them, "Tomorrow morning if you want a similar experience, ask the first ten people you meet in your organization what the purpose of your organization is and you'll find it's a very similar experience. They'll point all over the place." When people have a different sense of purpose and values, every decision that is made from then on is governed by those. There's no question that this is one of the fundamental causes of misalignment, low trust, interpersonal conflict, interdepartmental rivalry, people operating on personal agendas, and so forth.

Wright

Is that primarily a result of an inability to communicate from the top?

Covey

That's one aspect, but I think it's more fundamental. There's an inability to involve people—an unwillingness. Leaders may communicate what their mission and their strategy is, but that doesn't mean there's any emotional connection to it. Mission statements that are rushed and then announced are soon forgotten. They become nothing more than just a bunch of platitudes on the wall that mean essentially nothing and even create a source of cynicism and a sense of hypocrisy inside the culture of an organization.

Wright

How do companies ensure survival and prosperity in these tumultuous times of technological advances, mergers, downsizing, and change?

Covey

I think that it takes a lot of high trust in a culture that has something that doesn't change—principles—at its core. There are principles that people agree upon that are valued. It gives a sense of stability. Then you have the power to adapt and be flexible when you experience these kinds of disruptive new economic models or technologies that come in and sideswipe you. You don't know how to handle them unless you have something you can depend upon.

If people have not agreed to a common set of principles that guide them and a common purpose, then they get their security from the outside and they tend to freeze the structure, systems, and processes inside and they cease becoming adaptable. They don't change with the changing realities of the new marketplace out there and gradually they become obsolete.

Wright

I was interested in one portion of your book, *The 7 Habits of Highly Effective People,* where you talk about behaviors. How does an individual go about the process of replacing ineffective behaviors with effective ones?

Covey

I think that for most people it usually requires a crisis that humbles them to become aware of their ineffective behaviors. If there's not a crisis the tendency is to perpetuate those behaviors and not change.

You don't have to wait until the marketplace creates the crisis for you. Have everyone accountable on a 360-degree basis to everyone else they interact with—with feedback either formal or informal—where they are getting data as to what's happening. They will then start to realize that the consequences of their ineffective behavior require them to be humble enough to look at that behavior and to adopt new, more effective ways of doing things.

Sometimes people can be stirred up to this if you just appeal to their conscience—to their inward sense of what is right and wrong. A lot of people sometimes know inwardly they're doing wrong, but the culture doesn't necessarily discourage them from continuing that. They either need feedback from people or they need feedback from the marketplace or they need feedback from their conscience. Then they can begin to develop a step-by-step process of replacing old habits with new, better habits.

Wright

It's almost like saying, "Let's make all the mistakes in the laboratory before we put this thing in the air."

Covey

Right; and I also think what is necessary is a paradigm shift, which is analogous to having a correct map, say of a city or of a country. If people have an inaccurate paradigm of life, of other people, and of themselves it really doesn't make much difference what their behavior or habits or attitudes are. What they need is a correct paradigm—a correct map—that describes what's going on.

For instance, in the Middle Ages they used to heal people through bloodletting. It wasn't until Samuel Weiss and Pasteur and other empirical scientists discovered the germ theory that they realized for the first time they weren't dealing with the real issue. They realized why women preferred to use midwives who washed rather than doctors who didn't wash. They gradually got a new paradigm. Once you've got a new paradigm then your behavior and your attitude flow directly from it. If you have a bad paradigm or a bad map, let's say of a city, there's no way, no matter what your behavior or your habits or your attitudes are—how positive they are—you'll never be able to find the location you're looking for. This is why I believe that to change paradigms is far more fundamental than to work on attitude and behavior.

Wright

One of your seven habits of highly effective people is to "begin with the end in mind." If circumstances change and hardships or miscalculations occur, how does one view the end with clarity?

Covey

Many people think to begin with the end in mind means that you have some fixed definition of a goal that's accomplished and if changes come about you're not going to adapt to them. Instead, the "end in mind" you begin with is that you are going to create a flexible culture of high trust so that no matter what comes along you are going to do whatever it takes to accommodate that new change or that new reality and maintain a culture of high performance and high trust. You're talking more in terms of values and overall purposes that don't change, rather than specific strategies or programs that will have to change to accommodate the changing realities in the marketplace.

Wright

In this time of mistrust among people, corporations, and nations, for that matter, how do we create high levels of trust?

Covey

That's a great question and it's complicated because there are so many elements that go into the creating of a culture of trust. Obviously the most fundamental one is just to have trustworthy people. But that is not sufficient because what if the organization itself is misaligned?

For instance, what if you say you value cooperation but you really reward people for internal competition? Then you have a systemic or a structure problem that creates low trust inside the culture even though the people themselves are trustworthy. This is one of the insights of Edward Demming and the work he did. That's why he said that most problems are not personal—they're systemic. They're common caused. That's why you have to work on structure, systems, and processes to make sure that they institutionalize principle-centered values. Otherwise you could have good people with bad systems and you'll get bad results.

When it comes to developing interpersonal trust between people, it is made up of many, many elements such as taking the time to listen to other people, to understand them, and to see what is important to them. What we think is important to another may only be important to us, not to another. It takes empathy. You have to make and keep promises to them. You have to treat people with kindness and courtesy. You have to be completely honest and open. You have to live up to your commitments. You can't betray people behind their back. You can't badmouth them behind their back and sweet-talk them to their face. That will send out vibes of hypocrisy and it will be detected.

You have to learn to apologize when you make mistakes, to admit mistakes, and to also get feedback going in every direction as much as possible. It doesn't necessarily require formal forums—it requires trust between people who will be open with each other and give each other feedback.

Wright

My mother told me to do a lot of what you're saying now, but it seems that when I got in business I simply forgot.

Covey

Sometimes we forget, but sometimes culture doesn't nurture it. That's why I say unless you work with the institutionalizing—that means formalizing into structure, systems, and processing the values—you will not have a nurturing culture. You have to constantly work on that.

This is one of the big mistakes organizations make. They think trust is simply a function of being honest. That's only one small aspect. It's an important aspect, obviously, but there are so many other elements that go into the creation of a high-trust culture.

Wright

"Seek first to understand then to be understood" is another of your seven habits. Do you find that people try to communicate without really understanding what other people want?

Covey

Absolutely. The tendency is to project out of our own autobiography—our own life, our own value system—onto other people, thinking we know what they want. So we don't really listen to them. We pretend to listen, but we really don't listen from within their frame of reference. We listen from within our own frame of reference and we're really preparing our reply rather than seeking to understand. This is a very common thing. In fact, very few people have had any training in seriously listening. They're trained in how to read, write, and speak, but not to listen.

Reading, writing, speaking, and listening are the four modes of communication and they represent about two-thirds to three-fourths of our waking hours. About half of that time is spent listening, but it's the one skill people have not been trained in. People have had all this training in the other forms of communication. In a large audience of 1,000 people you wouldn't have more than twenty people who have had more than two weeks of training in listening. Listening is more than a skill or technique; you must listen within another's frame of reference. It takes tremendous courage to listen because you're at risk when you listen. You don't know what's going to happen; you're vulnerable.

Wright

Sales gurus always tell me that the number one skill in selling is listening.

Covey

Yes—listening from within the customer's frame of reference. That is so true. You can see that it takes some security to do that because you don't know what's going to happen.

Wright

With this book we're trying to encourage people to be better, to live better, and be more fulfilled by listening to the examples of our guest authors. Is there anything or anyone in your life that has made a difference for you and helped you to become a better person?

Covey

I think the most influential people in my life have been my parents. I think that what they modeled was not to make comparisons and harbor jealousy or to seek recognition. They were humble people.

I remember one time when my mother and I were going up in an elevator and the most prominent person in the state was also in the elevator. She knew him, but she spent her time talking to the elevator operator. I was just a little kid and I was so awed by the famous person. I said to her, "Why didn't you talk to the important person?" She said, "I was. I had never met him."

My parents were really humble, modest people who were focused on service and other people rather than on themselves. I think they were very inspiring models to me.

Wright

In almost every research paper I've ever read, those who write about people who have influenced their lives include three teachers in their top-five picks. My seventh-grade English teacher was the greatest teacher I ever had and she influenced me to no end.

Covey

Would it be correct to say that she saw in you probably some qualities of greatness you didn't even see in yourself?

Wright

Absolutely.

Covey

That's been my general experience—the key aspect of a mentor or a teacher is someone who sees in you potential that you don't even see in yourself. Those teachers/mentors treat you accordingly and eventually you come to see it in yourself. That's my definition of leadership or influence—communicating people's worth and potential so clearly that they are inspired to see it in themselves.

Wright

Most of my teachers treated me as a student, but she treated me with much more respect than that. As a matter of fact, she called me Mr. Wright, and I was in the seventh grade at the time. I'd never been addressed by anything but a nickname. I stood a little taller; she just made a tremendous difference.

Do you think there are other characteristics that mentors seem to have in common?

Covey

I think they are first of all good examples in their own personal lives. Their personal lives and their family lives are not all messed up—they come from a base of good character. They also are usually very confident and they take the time to do what your teacher did to you—to treat you with uncommon respect and courtesy.

They also, I think, explicitly teach principles rather than practices so that rules don't take the place of human judgment. You gradually come to have faith in your own judgment in making decisions because of the affirmation of such a mentor. Good mentors care about you—you can feel the sincerity of their caring. It's like the expression, "I don't care how much you know until I know how much you care."

Wright

Most people are fascinated with the new television shows about being a survivor. What has been the greatest comeback that you've made from adversity in your career or your life?

Covey

When I was in grade school I experienced a disease in my legs. It caused me to use crutches for a while. I tried to get off them fast and get back. The disease wasn't corrected yet so I went back on crutches for another year. The disease went to the other leg and I went on for another year. It essentially took me out of my favorite thing—

athletics—and it took me more into being a student. So that was a life-defining experience, which at the time seemed very negative, but has proven to be the basis on which I've focused my life—being more of a learner.

Wright

Principle-centered learning is basically what you do that's different from anybody I've read or listened to.

Covey

The concept is embodied in the Far Eastern expression, "Give a man a fish, you feed him for the day; teach him how to fish, you feed him for a lifetime." When you teach principles that are universal and timeless, they don't belong to just any one person's religion or to a particular culture or geography. They seem to be timeless and universal like the ones we've been talking about here: trustworthiness, honesty, caring, service, growth, and development. These are universal principles. If you focus on these things, then little by little people become independent of you and then they start to believe in themselves and their own judgment becomes better. You don't need as many rules. You don't need as much bureaucracy and as many controls and you can empower people.

The problem in most business operations today—and not just business but non-business—is that they're using the industrial model in an information age. Arnold Toynbee, the great historian, said, "You can pretty well summarize all of history in four words: nothing fails like success." The industrial model was based on the asset of the machine. The information model is based on the asset of the person—the knowledge worker. It's an altogether different model. But the machine model was the main asset of the twentieth century. It enabled productivity to increase fifty times. The new asset is intellectual and social capital—the qualities of people and the quality of the relationship they have with each other. Like Toynbee said, "Nothing fails like success." The industrial model does not work in an information age. It requires a focus on the new wealth, not capital and material things.

A good illustration that demonstrates how much we were into the industrial model, and still are, is to notice where people are on the balance sheet. They're not found there. Machines are found there. Machines become investments. People are on the profit-and-loss statement and people are expenses. Think of that—if that isn't bloodletting.

Wright

It sure is.

When you consider the choices you've made down through the years, has faith played an important role in your life?

Covey

It has played an extremely important role. I believe deeply that we should put principles at the center of our lives, but I believe that God is the source of those principles. I did not invent them. I get credit sometimes for some of the Seven Habits material and some of the other things I've done, but it's really all based on principles that have been given by God to all of His children from the beginning of time. You'll find that you can teach these same principles from the sacred texts and the wisdom literature of almost any tradition. I think the ultimate source of that is God and that is one thing you can absolutely depend upon—"in God we trust."

Wright

If you could have a platform and tell our audience something you feel would help them or encourage them, what would you say?

Covey

I think I would say to put God at the center of your life and then prioritize your family. No one on their deathbed ever wished they had spent more time at the office.

Wright

That's right. We have come down to the end of our program and I know you're a busy person. I could talk with you all day, Dr. Covey.

Covey

It's good to talk with you as well and to be a part of this program. It looks like an excellent one that you've got going on here.

Wright

Thank you.

We have been talking today with Dr. Stephen R. Covey, cofounder and vice-chairman of Franklin Covey Company. He's also the author of *The 7 Habits of Highly Effective People,* which has been ranked as a number one bestseller by the *New York Times,* selling more than fourteen million copies in thirty-eight languages.

Dr. Covey, thank you so much for being with us today.

Covey

Thank you for the honor of participating.

About the Author

Stephen R. Covey was recognized in 1996 as one of *Time* magazine's twenty-five most influential Americans and one of *Sales and Marketing Management's* top twenty-five power brokers. Dr. Covey is the author of several acclaimed books, including the international bestseller, *The 7 Habits of Highly Effective People*, named the number one Most Influential Business Book of the Twentieth Century, and other best sellers that include *First Things First, Principle-Centered Leadership,* (with sales exceeding one million) and *The 7 Habits of Highly Effective Families.*

Dr. Covey's newest book, *The 8th Habit: From Effectiveness to Greatness*, which was released in November 2004, rose to the top of several bestseller lists, including *New York Times, Wall Street Journal, USA Today, Money, Business Week*, Amazon.com, and Barnes & Noble.

Dr. Covey earned his undergraduate degree from the University of Utah, his MBA from Harvard, and completed his doctorate at Brigham Young University. While at Brigham Young University, he served as assistant to the President and was also a professor of Business Management and Organizational Behavior. He received the National Fatherhood Award in 2003, which, as the father of nine and grandfather of forty-four, he says is the most meaningful award he has ever received.

Dr. Covey currently serves on the board of directors for the Points of Light Foundation. Based in Washington, D.C., the Foundation, through its partnership with the Volunteer Center National Network, engages and mobilizes millions of volunteers from all walks of life—businesses, nonprofits, faith-based organizations, low-income communities, families, youth, and older adults—to help solve serious social problems in thousands of communities.

Dr. Stephen R. Covey
www.stephencovey.com

An Interview with…

Jeff Wolf

Chapter Two

An interview with…

Jeff Wolf

David E. Wright (Wright)

Our guest today is Jeff Wolf, one of America's most dynamic speakers, one of the country's top executive coaches, and a highly sought-after business consultant. His strategic focus in solving corporate and human challenges has garnered continuing raves from national firms. He has been featured on NBC and FOX TV, has authored the upcoming book, *The Essence of Effective Leadership,* and has worked with many of the world's largest corporations.

Jeff is the former CEO of one of the country's largest healthcare receivables management companies, as well as one of the most prestigious polling and political opinion research corporations. As a successful basketball coach, Jeff was selected by Gillette as one of the country's outstanding coaches, and he appeared nationally on radio and television shows to promote leadership, teamwork, and positive attitudes.

Jeff is currently president of Wolf Management Consultants, one of the most comprehensive consulting, training, and coaching firms in the country. The firm specializes in helping people, teams, and organizations achieve maximum effectiveness. Throughout the years,

Jeff has been lauded as a respected authority on leadership. His principles, strategies, and inspiration have influenced dramatic growth and changes in countless organizations.

Jeff, welcome to *Roadmap to Success!*

Jeff Wolf (Wolf)

Thank you, David. It's good to be here.

Wright

Jeff, you have a broad perspective on leadership. How would you describe what it takes to become a great leader?

Wolf

David, three areas immediately come to mind:

1. Number one is honesty. Today's leaders must be honest, forthright, and "ooze" integrity. People want their leaders to be role models whose allegiances and priorities are beyond reproach. Sadly, over the last few years, we've seen far too many leaders who lied and manipulated people, finances, and processes to fit their own needs. When we read newspaper headlines or surf the Web, we regularly learn about politicians, businesses, and corporate executives who have been incredibly dishonest—and the results have been catastrophic. Companies like Andersen and Enron have closed, leaving many innocent people in the lurch. Their life savings have been wiped out, and careers have been sabotaged.

   Leaders must have a strong character and integrity, which means "walking the walk" and "talking the talk." The moment leaders bend the truth, they lose their credibility—and they'll never get it back.

2. Leadership is all about people. About forty years ago, Walt Disney said, "You can dream, create, and design the most wonderful place in the world, but it takes people to make the dream a reality." I think

it's safe to say that when Disney made this statement, he probably never imagined how prophetic his words would be. Regardless of one's type of business—blue collar or white collar—or the organization's size, people make a company. Without highly motivated and inspired employees, an organization will struggle to survive and thrive.

Motivated people provide a competitive advantage. As a leader, you can make the difference between having great people who are motivated and go to the nth degree to meet their responsibilities or you can be stuck with people who show up for work every day (if you're lucky) and merely go through the motions while collecting a paycheck. Great leaders motivate people to work together and achieve greatness, and they instill confidence and earn employees' trust—a commodity that can never be bought.

Another critical role is nurturing the growth and development of other leaders within the organization. The more leaders you create at every level, the more successful the organization will be. You don't have to look any further than Jack Welch at GE, who strongly believed in growing leaders at every level and committed an enormous amount of time and money to training and developing them. This strategy allowed him to build a much stronger company.

3. Finally, no leader can succeed without a clear, compelling, and inspiring vision, which must be communicated in a way that everyone understands. Only then will people be motivated and inspired to work as a team toward common goals.

    Leaders must clearly define and paint an exciting path to the future, while providing fundamental, ethical, and logical reasons as to why they're moving in a specific direction. They must articulate a clear framework and provide a very cogent message that delineates each individual's role in realizing the vision. This builds support and enthusiasm, creating an environment where people are aligned and eager to participate in achieving company goals.

Leaders must also create excitement and spark people's imaginations of what the future holds. When strategies, objectives, and paths to success are clearly defined, individuals, teams, and the organization as a whole will be motivated, inspired, and energized.

Wright

Now, let's turn this around. How would you define a poor leader?

Wolf

Studies have shown that the number one reason people leave organizations is the boss! This is an unfortunate commentary on the state of leadership in the twenty-first century. Some characteristics of a poor leader include:

- The need to control and create an atmosphere of negativity, coupled with rare or no praise and recognition.
- The inability to keep one's word, poor treatment of people, taking credit for others' successes, and a habit of blaming others for one's personal failures.
- To make matters worse, poor leaders may cover up mistakes they have made—a behavior that usually results in high turnover and a lack of engagement by those who stay.
- Poor leaders fail to delegate or empower people. Instead, they micromanage others' work. Their inability or refusal to develop an atmosphere of trust deprives people of opportunities to grow and gain the confidence necessary to succeed. By controlling people and undermining them in front of their peers, these leaders ultimately damage their companies. If this behavior goes unchecked, there may be a point of no return that destroys a once productive company.
- One common phenomenon is employee promotion based on technical know-how, high performance, or attrition. These individuals are frequently thrown into the leadership role without any kind of basic training—not even a management boot camp. Is it

any wonder they're criticized for underperformance? Let's face it: We'd never expect a poorly trained physician to cure us. How, then, can the business world expect ill-equipped leaders to lead without appropriate training? We set them up for failure, and a formerly top-notch employee, through no fault of his or her own, suddenly becomes an albatross.

That said, it's important to emphasize that poor leadership is usually correctable if swift action is taken.

Wright

Good point. So let's talk about leadership as a learnable skill. We know the art of leadership can be learned. What advice do you have for those who lack a natural aptitude and require ongoing practice to become effective?

Wolf

As you've correctly stated, leadership is indeed a skill, and most leaders aren't born with extraordinary abilities; rather, they develop their skill sets by learning, practicing, and refining them on a daily basis. Just as a competitive athlete trains to win, leaders must commit to work hard, adopt a positive attitude, and demonstrate a desire for constant learning. They must also understand their leadership style will change over time and, as circumstances dictate, remain flexible.

I would encourage budding and aspiring leaders to create a plan, put it in writing, and then "work it." Research proves that people who put their goals in writing are usually more successful.

Read as many books and attend as many training courses as possible, both within and outside of the company. Vary courses so you can experience a broad spectrum of leadership skills.

There's another important challenge to overcome: Learn the areas in which you must improve because we all have blind spots. We see some of our weaknesses, but it's truly impossible to identify all of them. Working with a coach is a powerful way to improve your leadership skills. Under the right circumstances, one-on-one coaching with an objective third party can provide support that other training methods simply cannot. Coaches are attuned to one's unique individual needs.

Also learn what your company looks for in its leaders. See if there's a competency model that identifies successful leaders' strengths and characteristics. Study this model and be sure to practice the competencies. If no such model exists, seek out successful company leaders and talk with them to gain a better understanding of how they became successful.

You should also volunteer to lead small projects, which will provide useful leadership experiences. You'll gain confidence and enhance the skill sets that are weak.

Use 360-degree feedback and other assessment tools to identify leadership competencies and skills. This provides a valid measure of the areas that require work. Leaders must understand how their behavior is perceived by others to effectively change their behavior, and 360-degree feedback often solves this problem.

Lastly, always be curious. Seek new opportunities and experiences, and always be open to trying something out of your normal comfort zone.

Wright

Assessing, training, and coaching—all of these important functions place leaders in situations that allow them to succeed and gain confidence. To follow up, what are the initial steps organizations need to take to develop effective leaders?

Wolf

Effective leadership programs must be designed, developed, and implemented to teach the essence of leadership skills and behaviors required in today's competitive business environment. Programs must be driven by business needs and designed to enhance capabilities for current and future leaders.

A leadership program must be tied to existing company values, and the skills and behaviors to be taught should support them. In addition, the program should build on a set of leadership competencies that are unique to the organization.

Wright

How do you convince senior-level executives to commit to ongoing development for middle- and upper-level leaders?

Wolf

It definitely starts at the top with senior-level commitment. Research shows that failure to begin developing current and future leaders (not to mention creating a strategic succession plan) results in a company's inability to compete and ultimately survive. As we all know, Baby Boomers, who comprise most upper- and mid-level managers, are transitioning out of the workforce. Data shows a severe shortage of skilled people coming in to take their place. So, what senior management in today's organizations needs to do is move quickly, with a strategic succession plan to grow and nurture existing and new talent. Otherwise, the organization is doomed to fail.

The other day, I was talking to an executive in a Fortune 100 Company who told me how critical the next several years will be for his company to grow its bench strength, as they are going to lose approximately 30 percent of their key people to retirement. For this organization, as with others, it comes down to a strategic organizational initiative to implement leadership development programs immediately.

David, in the last two years, our company has had more requests for leadership development programs than we've had in the previous six years combined. Programs are not designed strictly for upper- and mid-level management, but also for high-potential individuals and supervisory-level employees. We have developed numerous successful programs for every level. When leaders finish them and master leadership skills, they're ready to take a quantum leap up the leadership ladder.

Wright

On which areas do you focus in these programs?

Wolf

There are many areas of focus, but we initially work very hard to customize a program to fit organizations' and participants' specific needs. We interview stakeholders and all participants prior to designing the program to acquire an understanding of current leadership knowledge and skill level. We then integrate the organizational culture, views, and philosophy into the program.

Generally speaking, we focus on core areas such as:

- Creating and driving a vision
- Building and managing relationships
- Becoming a strategic thinker
- Demonstrating deep business knowledge
- Solving problems
- Making decisions
- Achieving results
- Communicating and listening effectively
- Coaching
- Empowering people
- Developing performance goals and standards
- Providing performance feedback
- Building strong teams and team dynamics
- Executing tasks
- Managing conflict
- Leading change
- Engaging employees
- Developing talent

Wright

That is a tremendous amount of material to cover. How long do these programs usually last, and what format do you use?

Wolf

It varies, but programs can last anywhere from three to twelve months. Structure and format depend on an organization's needs, desired outcomes, and participants' skill levels. For example, one company identified seventy-five high-potential leaders. We designed and developed three programs with twenty-five participants each. They lasted six months and involved three components: a series of monthly workshops, one-on-one coaching, and a leadership project in which they recruited and led a team to put learned skills into practice in real time. At the end of six months, each participant had to present project results to fellow classmates and describe in detail the pitfalls, challenges, and rewards faced along the way.

Another program we designed involved upper-level executives. We held a series of biweekly three-hour evening programs that ran for nine months and included one-on-one coaching.

A third program involved twenty participants from the same company, but from different locations around the country. We kicked off the program in person, with all participants in attendance, and we explained the curriculum, objectives, and expectations. Thereafter, every week for thirteen consecutive weeks, we held one-hour group teleconferences to discuss various leadership topics. I also coached each person during this time to reinforce identified skills.

As you can see, each program was unique, depending on each organization's particular needs.

Wright

All of these examples have a coaching component. Do you include one in all of your leadership development programs?

Wolf

Yes. What we're trying to do is change behavior. In general, people will attend training programs and learn many new ideas and skills. But as soon as they return to their offices, they're hit from all sides with client issues, personnel problems, and every other conceivable situation. As a result, they have no time to fully digest and practice what they learned, and program content is often forgotten.

We want to accomplish two goals in every leadership development program: change participants' behavior and make newly learned skills part of their everyday work habits. Changing an old habit and developing a new one takes time. That's where coaching comes in. It reinforces training by working one-on-one with each person to abandon bad habits and adopt the more positive ones learned during training. Participants can then discuss what's working—and not working—with their coach in complete confidence. The coach will hold them accountable and be there for support when needed, which proves extremely valuable.

One interesting study tracked executives who participated in a leadership development program, followed by eight weeks of one-on-one coaching. The study found that training alone increased leadership productivity by 22.4 percent, while coaching and training increased productivity by 88 percent.

So, you see, David, we are firm believers that the combination of coaching and training is critical to running a successful program with a high return on investment.

Wright

If I'm a leader, how can I develop the people who report directly to me so they can assume more responsibility?

Wolf

One of the most important leadership roles is nurturing other leaders' growth and development within the organization. To develop people to take on more responsibility, a leader must support, encourage, and coach people so they can cultivate new skills and embrace opportunities for professional development and personal growth. Leaders must guide and encourage others to create their own development plans, not do it for them. People are more productive when they take ownership of their plans.

Next, you have to set expectations, encourage people to achieve their goals, praise their successes often, and ensure the flow of open communication.

Leaders must continually challenge, probe, and ask questions to teach sound decision-making. These questions have to be open-ended, not yes or no. Great questions include the following:

- How does that work?
- What does that mean?
- If you do this, what do you think may happen?
- Why do you think it will work?
- What's your next step?
- Which tools do you need?

These questions teach people to become analytical and think more strategically.

Lastly, you must empower people by giving them ownership, which demonstrates your confidence in their abilities and allows them to succeed or fail on their own.

Wright

In your experiences as a CEO, executive coach, and consultant, how do you identify high-potential new leaders?

Wolf

Leaders must be proficient in both hard and soft skills. For years, organizations looked at only hard skills or technical knowledge, such as expertise in strategy or finance. They viewed these skills as the most important characteristics of high-potential leaders. Today, however, the soft skills, which we also call people or interpersonal skills, cannot be overlooked when we're looking for the next generation of leaders.

It's very rewarding to see how many of the elite MBA programs are now including soft skills in their curricula! In today's world, soft skills are some of, if not *the* most important, attributes a leader can have. If leaders want to have successors, they must build alignment and influence people, create strong teams, earn loyalty, remain positive, motivate people, and have great listening skills. Each of these is a soft skill—and without them, you'll fail as a leader.

Taking the hard skills for granted, the necessary soft skills to look for include:

- Effective communication
- Coaching
- Good listening skills
- The ability to build effective and cohesive teams
- The ability to build relationships with their own staffs and teams, as well as with cross-functional areas, to accomplish goals and get work done
- A sense of inquisitiveness, a willingness to improve, and a tendency to ask a lot of questions
- An understanding of how their actions have an effect not only on themselves, but also on others

Leadership is both difficult and demanding because leaders must help drive results, inspire, guide people and teams, and make tough decisions. Clearly, not everyone has the desire to lead, so I also ask the following questions:

- Does the person want to be a leader?
- What are his or her goals and aspirations?

- Do individuals see the big picture versus having a "silo mentality"?
- Are they problem-solvers? Do they have the ability to strategically navigate complicated issues?
- What types of real-life experiences do they have?
- Are they honest and ethical?

It's important for leaders to be positive and have a great attitude because they can either impart or sap energy. A leader's upbeat attitude becomes contagious, lifting the morale of those around him or her. You can always teach skills, but you cannot always teach people how to be positive; they either have a great attitude or they don't.

Observe firsthand how potential leaders work with others and how other people view them. When they stand up to speak in front of a group, do they exude confidence, present articulate, clear messages, and carry themselves well? They should also have good judgment skills in three discrete areas:

- **People.** Can they make sound judgments about people, such as anticipating the need for key personnel changes and aligning people to make the right call?
- **Strategy.** Are they flexible and adaptable? Can they make changes when a current strategy isn't working?
- **Grace Under Pressure.** When they're in crisis situations, do they remain calm, focus on their goals, think clearly, and develop new alternative strategies? When they make a mistake, do they admit it, let others know about it, and move forward, or do they try to hide it? By admitting mistakes, they serve as role models, communicating that it's okay to fail and make a mistake.

Lastly, leaders should employ a series of tests and assessments to further measure hard and soft skills.

Wright

When you identify, groom, and promote your most talented high performers, what's the best way to retain them?

Wolf

Retaining high-performing individuals is one of the most difficult problems facing organizations today. There's a war for talent, and most organizations are losing it as headhunters and competitors vie for the most accomplished candidates. What makes retention even more challenging is our mobile society: Top performers may not even think twice about leaving.

Great organizations view employee retention as a competitive advantage and they work hard to retain their most talented people. They understand that talented people are their most important asset.

Retention starts with culture. If you want to keep your top talent, you must create an inspiring and energizing culture wherein they can thrive. This means having an organization with shared values, openness, and honesty, thereby creating trust and allowing talented people to voice their opinions and share ideas.

You must empower and encourage people to aspire to do great things and be innovative, and then you reward their successes. High performers want to be challenged, provided with interesting work, and have the ability to make a difference. Leaders must recognize that everyone is motivated in different ways and they should take the time to find out what motivates each person. If you can pinpoint these motivators, you can work with your staff to achieve extraordinary results.

Continually praise and recognize individual achievements, and make people feel good about themselves and their accomplishments. Be accessible, listen to their suggestions and ideas, and keep them informed of everything that affects them.

Be certain you place them in the right positions. All too often we place people in jobs for which they're not suited. A specific job may not be challenging enough or individuals may lack the required skill sets. We always want to make sure the fit is correct.

Every leader must be held accountable for retaining talented people. If you see a pattern of turnover under a specific leader, a red flag should go up. Talented people will not put up with ineffective leaders.

Continually look for signs of dissatisfaction. Asking questions and receiving feedback are great ways to find out if people's needs are being met. Leaders should ask their high performers questions like:

- What can we do to make you happier here?
- If the organization could stop doing one thing, what would it be?
- What's challenging about your work?
- What motivates you to work harder?
- What are the greatest obstacles to getting your work done?
- What resources do you need that you currently lack?

These questions will open a constructive dialogue that allows you to discover talented people's needs. Once you gain awareness, you must work quickly to fulfill these needs.

Lastly, provide continual education and training so leaders can grow and learn new ideas. Then provide a career path with opportunities for growth and advancement.

Wright

How do you fully engage people and earn their commitment on an ongoing basis?

Wolf

High on the list of what people want most from their leaders are praise, recognition, and appreciation. Research shows that appreciation is one of the most important ways people become engaged and motivated, and it improves overall morale. People need to feel respected and important, and they want to enjoy a sense of accomplishment. Effective leaders try to "catch people doing something right," and they rely on an arsenal of positive phrases such as: You're doing a great job on the Jones account; thanks for turning in your report early; and, you really made a difference in the project's success! It's amazing how much influence an encouraging leader has on individuals' performance! When people believe in themselves, they can accomplish great things.

As I mentioned earlier, people want to work for a company that has a culture of high values, ethics, and honesty. The culture should include open communication. As Wal-Mart founder Sam Walton once said, "Communicate everything to your associates. The more they know, the more they care, and once they care, there is no stopping them." People need to be kept informed about what's happening within the organization, their teams, and departments.

Training is another key to keeping people engaged and motivated. By encouraging and promoting ongoing training and development, you create a pipeline of talented people who are full of ideas, thoughts, and inspiration. This will make your organization very successful, and it also sends a very strong, motivating message to each employee: We care and we're willing to invest in you. You'll then be rewarded with a tremendous amount of engagement and enthusiasm, which positions your organization as an employer of choice.

Coaching also plays an important role in keeping people engaged and committed. It brings out the best in them and helps remove obstacles to their success. Coaching is not about telling people what to do or how to do it; rather, you want to help them discover their own path by encouraging and questioning. It's important to ask questions like:

- With which past projects did you struggle?

- What steps will you take to accomplish your goals?
- What excuses are you making?
- What's holding you back?
- What have you tried since the last time we talked?

Open-ended questions make people think through obstacles. More importantly, coaching shows that you care and are willing to share yourself with them.

Another important way to keep people motivated, engaged, and committed is to make the workplace an enjoyable, fun place to be each day.

Wright

In the fast-paced world of business, fun and work often seem to be an oxymoron. Why is having fun so important?

Wolf

David, I'm a firm believer in loving what you do and that life's too short to settle for a job you don't like. When I speak to audiences across the country, I often ask the following question: "How many of you love what you're doing?" It never fails to amaze me that only about 20 to 25 percent of audience members raise their hands. And those who don't stare in awe at them!

What does this tell us about the state of the workforce today? Well, a recent Gallup poll revealed that 70 percent of the workforce is disengaged, and the longer they stay with a company, the more disengaged they become. If people wake up every day and aren't excited and energized about going to work, something must be done to change this. After all, the average worker spends one-third of his or her time at work. An *Industry Week* poll found that 63 percent of employees find work anything but fun. This is a distressing revelation.

Fun in the workplace must be part of an organization's overall strategy. People should not only work hard, but they should also have fun. These are not mutually exclusive concepts, and the organization must embrace this principle. Are you aware that some companies have two CFOs: the traditional chief financial officer and the chief fun officer, who's responsible for creating ways for people to have fun at work? Just remember one thing: People rarely succeed at anything unless they have fun doing it.

Just look at the list of companies that make fun part of their corporate strategic plan and culture:

- Southwest Airlines
- Starbucks
- Disney
- Nordstrom
- Wal-Mart
- Trader Joe's
- Land's End

Now, what else do these organizations have in common? The answer: They're all very profitable! I can think of four specific benefits for businesses that encourage fun:

1. Fun is a healer. When people are having fun, the brain releases chemicals called endorphins that help heal the body. This reduces absenteeism and helps keep people healthy and happy each day.

2. Fun breeds creativity and new ideas. As people enjoy their jobs and have fun, they become more creative and imaginative. They begin to think outside the box and will not fear failure.

3. Fun helps maintain workplace relations. America has the most diverse workforce in its history. People come to work every day with different cultural backgrounds. We also have a multigenerational workforce: people in their twenties to those in their sixties. And

when they're having fun at work, it breaks down barriers. They enjoy being with each other, can discuss their differences openly, and share new ideas.

4. When you have fun at work, it makes training and teaching easier. In fact, fun is an excellent teaching tool. Whenever our company holds workshops or conducts training, we make sure to include strategically placed activities that focus on fun. The feedback we always receive is positive. Participants say they learned a lot and had fun doing it!

Having fun at work also has a major impact on the bottom line:

- Fun breeds creativity, prompting energy levels to rise.
- Energy is contagious and productivity soars.
- As the company enjoys increased productivity, there's greater innovation. New ideas and concepts take flight and the bottom line improves considerably.

I recently flew on Southwest Airlines for the first time, and I was amazed by every employee's high energy and enthusiasm—without exception. Each one was having fun and enjoying their work, from the baggage handlers, reservation agents, and gate attendants all the way up to the pilot. As I waited for my flight, I observed how the employees' positive attitudes and infectious enthusiasm spread to the passengers. Everyone was smiling, upbeat, and having a good time.

No wonder Southwest is so profitable at a time when many other airlines are struggling. Having fun at work makes a huge difference!

Wright

Another major leadership issue is communication and information-sharing. How does a leader remember to keep people in the loop so they can perform their jobs most efficiently?

Wolf

I always say, "Communicate, communicate, communicate, communicate—and then communicate even more!" You must have open lines of communication up and down all levels of the organization. I believe in the KISS principle: "Keep it simple, stupid" or "Keep it short and sweet." Simple things move through an organization faster, eliminate clutter, and reflect greater clarity.

When communicating, leaders must use different formats to get their message across: newsletters, e-mails, one-on-one or group meetings, and town halls. The most important goal is clarity. Often, leaders know what they want to communicate, but they fail to communicate clearly. When speaking, our tone of voice or inflections may have different meanings to people from diverse backgrounds and levels of experience. As such, it's incumbent upon leaders to communicate in a way that's clearly understood, without confusion, ambiguity, or misinterpretation.

Communication is one reason so many initiatives fail. It's so important to think carefully about how you express yourself, and it's best to develop a communication plan. How you communicate with people will vary, depending on the recipients and their positions in the organization, the parts of the initiative you want to share with them, and the timing of the communication.

Leaders and organizations can never take communication for granted, and they need to think of it as a product. This requires them to take an occasional communication inventory: looking at all current channels, vehicles, systems, and networks to find out who communicates to whom. Then, analyze the communication system and make it as effective as you would any other system in the organization.

Wright

Communication is such a complex topic, affecting the leadership gamut—those who are just moving into leadership positions, leaders in the midst of significant organizational change, and even the most experienced leaders. One question that comes up quite often deals with communication style: How can I be a firm leader, but still be liked and respected by my staff?

Wolf

Interesting question! A new leader usually assumes a position of responsibility, and his or her first inclination is to become too friendly with people. After all, everyone wants to be liked. But by trying to become everyone's friend, leaders run the risk of losing respect and influence. If your staff considers you to be one of the group, they may not respect your judgment on important issues.

Additionally, they may lose their motivation to achieve goals, fail to work hard, and assume deadlines are soft when they believe their "friend" will never reprimand them. That's why leaders must avoid falling into the trap of becoming too friendly with their staff. The bottom line? You're the boss—not a best friend! You cannot be objective and unbiased when staff members view you as a work pal.

Wright

Difficult employees can upset the equilibrium in even the most well-run business environments. How can leaders deal with them effectively?

Wolf

Unfortunately, many leaders steer clear of dealing with difficult people in the workplace, thereby contributing to conflict through avoidance. There will always be difficult employees, regardless of organizational level or the position an employee holds. People problems are often the most challenging and time-consuming parts of a leader's job.

Often, people are difficult because they may not know any other type of behavior or because no one has ever told them their behavior is inappropriate. Either way, when behavior poses a problem, leaders must deal with it quickly. The longer you wait, the worse the situation usually becomes. Failure to act swiftly can have a devastating effect on other employees. They may become upset, unproductive, and suffer low morale. If one person's negative behavior persists long enough without a resolution, good employees may ultimately get fed up and leave. As a businessperson, you can't afford to risk this.

The leader's goal is to find a solution by staying focused on the problem and not attacking the person causing it. Instead, point out specific examples of his or her objectionable behavior. Encourage the individual to talk and be honest with you by asking open-ended, leading questions. Avoid questions that can be answered with a simple yes or no. Then, listen carefully to what's being said. The more probing you can do, the better your chance of identifying the real source of the problems.

Become an active listener. Paraphrase key points the other person is making. For example, say: "What I hear you saying is—" and repeat what the person has told you. Let the individual acknowledge whether what you heard is right or wrong so you're on the same page. Remember: You want to uncover the reasons for the behavior, so don't interrupt when the person is speaking and remain nonjudgmental.

Once you determine the source of the problem, work together to create opportunities to find solutions that correct behavior. Make sure the person comes up with some of these solutions on his or her own, which allows ownership in remedying the problem and gives people a vested interest in the outcome. Then, create an action plan that holds the person accountable for future behavior problems. Accountability is vital: If the behavior continues—and depending on its severity—you'll need to determine when and how to handle follow-up counseling. And if the behavioral changes fail to occur, possible termination is the next step.

Here's a good roadmap for handling difficult behavior:

- Determine the problem
- Identify the reasons for it

- Generate options
- Evaluate these options
- Create an action plan that focuses on accountability
- Follow through on the plan

Difficult employees should never be surprised if termination occurs. From a legal and HR perspective, you must document every counseling and disciplinary meeting where you've outlined the expected goals and consequences for failing to meet them. After verbal warnings, make sure you progress to written warnings when negative behavior continues. And after several written warnings, make sure employees understand that their jobs are now on the line.

Wright

You spoke earlier about leaders needing to embrace change. With this in mind, how can they lead change initiatives without upsetting morale?

Wolf

In today's business environment, change is necessary. Business conditions are constantly changing, and yesterday's practices may no longer work. Leaders have to be flexible and adaptable to adjust to shifting business climates, but it's very important for them to understand that "leading change" is more than just a process.

We often forget that the most important aspects of change are people and their morale. It's often very easy to strategically manage the process and erroneously believe that when we have the correct process in place, change will automatically work. We frequently forget that change is very emotional for the average employee. As leaders, we need to understand the emotional process people experience and the impact it has on morale. One of the most natural human instincts is to resist change, even if it's beneficial.

There are really only two ways to look at change. First, change is constant. Second, change is upsetting. When any significant change occurs in an organization, stress becomes a given. Expect to see plenty of discomfort and even resentment, regardless of people's level of acceptance.

If not properly led, change can negatively affect individual and organizational performance. Consequences may include a negative environment as well as decreased performance and increased stress. Even when it's clearly evident that change is working, it's often difficult to keep morale at a healthy level. For this reason, leaders must understand the four phases most people go through when attempting to adapt to change:

1. The first phase is resistance. We are all creatures of habit, and when change happens, we are forcing people out of their comfort zones. As such, they will usually fight it. They may feel their needs were already being met and that the new changes will make it difficult to fulfill their needs. They may also fear the change will ultimately fail. At this point, people will probably do just enough to get by.

    At this stage people also have a very difficult time leaving the past behind them. They are so invested and have often been extremely successful in the old ways of doing things; now they're being asked to move out of their comfort zones and learn new ways. Leaders must therefore understand that people need time to mourn and let go of the past. They should listen carefully to what people are saying; more importantly, listen to what they're not saying.

    Leaders must be highly visible and available to answer questions, offer support, and be consistent in their messages. And in this resistance stage, leaders must be optimistic and serve as role models for change.

2. The second phase of change is confusion. Many people enjoy being the bearer of bad news. During this phase, rumors run rampant. People feel things are happening too fast and they don't know where

to focus their energy. They have problems learning new skills and will start finger-pointing at management. It was management who "created the mess," right? So, expect people to be highly stressed, with some even coming close to burning out.

As leaders, we must again be consistent in our messages and communications, and we should set short-term goals that can be accomplished and celebrated. Create incentives to maintain momentum as change occurs, and regularly restate the vision of where the company is headed.

3. The third phase is integration. People will begin taking ownership; there is more positive and less negative energy. People start to experience a sense of control, and there's some blossoming optimism.

    As leaders, we must provide encouragement and keep the lines of communication open. Encourage people to be creative, focused, and willing to share their ideas and feedback.

4. The final phase is commitment. There is now much less stress and increased productivity. People begin to take ownership, and there's acceptance of the change. Everyone appears to be on the same page, there is an increase in productivity, and the lines of communication are open. People feel good about themselves and the accomplishments they have achieved during the difficult change process.

As leaders, we have to celebrate successes and continually encourage, reward, and recognize high performance. We have to remain patient, as change doesn't happen overnight. It takes time.

As for morale, always respect the past. It served you well over the years. But you don't want to continually look in the rearview mirror. Focus on moving forward.

Wright

You've talked about coaching people through the change process. Let's shift gears and talk about coaching. You have successfully coached hundreds of executives and are considered one of the top business coaches in the country. What advice would you offer leaders about the importance of coaching their people?

Wolf

Coaching is one of the most important leadership duties and responsibilities. When leaders take the time to coach, people become more confident and motivated, which leads to higher performance and productivity. Leaders build relationships on trust and encouragement, and they need to support people so they can "be all they can be," to coin a phrase from U.S. Army recruiters. Research studies demonstrate that organizations with a strong coaching culture develop much higher levels of employee engagement and performance.

Leaders must understand that coaching is a powerful tool. It helps people overcome obstacles to their success. As a leader, you must take the time to get to know your people because coaching is based on trust and confidence. The coaching process will bring to the forefront:

- At what do people excel?
- What are their weaknesses?
- What's their potential?
- What are their limitations?
- Where do they want to go in their careers?

When leaders can answer these questions, they can structure jobs within the work environment and provide the feedback required to enhance performance. This allows people to find their roadmap to success and provides appropriate resources and training.

The best piece of advice I can give is this: Coaching is not about providing the answers. It's a process of using questions, active listening, and support to help people achieve a higher level of success. Coaches ask the right questions to move people to what I call the "ah-ha" moment. This occurs when people being coached figure something out and realize they have found the answer. The leader didn't give them the answers, but asked leading questions to help them find it. This is what makes coaching so powerful.

Active listening means giving your total attention to the person you're coaching. This is critical. You need to hear what the person is saying and not saying. This skill may prove difficult for some leaders because active listening requires them to suspend judgment and carefully tune into what the other person is saying and feeling.

Coaching opens lines of communication to create a comfortable environment where performance issues can be discussed freely and without defensiveness.

Leaders who are effective coaches have more successful teams, higher morale and, in most cases, better bottom-line results. The benefits of coaching are numerous:

- Improved trust and morale because people know they're being heard
- Improved performance, with people developing skills and abilities as the coach encourages them to find new and better ways to accomplish tasks and goals
- Higher productivity and more confident, motivated people
- Better customer service
- Higher retention of key people
- Less stress
- People who can reach their full potential

Organizations are focusing on coaching for several key reasons:

- People are your key source of competitive advantage.
- They have to be adaptable and flexible.

- We have to do more with less.
- Maintaining a high-performance work culture is key to survival.

Coaching provides these benefits and many more.

Wright

Does coaching take a lot of time?

Wolf

Not at all, David. One of its many benefits is that it doesn't always have to be conducted in formal sessions. Coaching may be as simple as walking over to a person's desk and asking how things are going or having a short chat in the hallway.

I find it interesting that organizations will invest millions of dollars in equipment, hold weeks and months of meetings, and spend an inordinate amount of time making a decision, but they shortsightedly won't invest the same time and money in coaching their people! Let's get real: People are your human capital and most valuable assets. If leaders invest the appropriate time and money in coaching, people will be more productive and motivated, and the organization will show better bottom-line results. One University of Pennsylvania study found that spending 10 percent of revenue on capital improvements boosts productivity by 3.9 percent. A similar investment in developing human capital increases productivity by 8.5 percent—more than double the gain.

So, if leaders spend time coaching people, there are obvious benefits to the organization.

Wright

External coaching is widely used in organizations today, and you are the person brought in to coach their leaders. Why is there so much need for such coaching and what are the most common areas that require improvement?

Wolf

Coaching used to be thought of as a tool to help correct underperformance or, as I often call it, the "broken wing theory." Today, coaching is used to support leaders, employees with high potential, and top producers in an effort to enhance individual capabilities.

We work in such a high-speed environment! Organizations are finally beginning to recognize the importance of helping leaders achieve critical business objectives in the shortest possible time, so they're hiring coaches to speed personnel development. What's so unique about coaching is its inherent ability to provide opportunities to learn on the job without removing leaders from their day-to-day responsibilities. It's efficient, cost-effective, and more beneficial than being a passive participant at a four-hour lecture, where one is likely to retain less than 20 percent of the material covered. And coaching is specifically tailored to individuals' needs, so time isn't wasted on areas where participants already excel.

I'd like to share a story that illustrates my point. A few weeks ago, I followed Tiger Woods for several holes at the Buick Invitational Tournament, and I marveled at his concentration and skills. I asked myself: Does Tiger Woods need a coach to be a great golfer? The answer is probably no. But has he become a *better* golfer by working with a coach? The answer is a resounding yes! In Tiger's case, coaching helps him succeed beyond current levels and elevates his game. It's not intended to fix a problem. The same applies to coaching top leaders who cling to some bad habits. A qualified coach can turn an excellent leader into a true powerhouse.

I'm often brought into organizations to deal with a number of leadership issues. Providing feedback is one key area. As executives move into greater levels of responsibility, they receive less—perhaps even no—feedback from others on their performance. The unfortunate consequence is stagnation. Critical leadership and interpersonal skills often reach certain levels, and the executive is given no opportunity to become an even better leader. Working one-on-one with an objective third-party coach offers these leaders a trusted advisor who can focus on behavioral changes that organizations are ill equipped to handle.

The most common leadership areas that require improvement include the following:

- Improving poor communication skills
- Building job-critical competencies
- Changing executive behavior to create a positive, long-term impact on the organization
- Indecisiveness
- Leading a multigenerational workplace
- Effectively managing stress and burnout
- Sharpening high-potential individuals' skills
- Increasing productivity
- Building strong and effective teams
- Resolving conflict
- Making goals congruent with the organization's or company's mission
- Fear of failure or success
- Time management skills
- Lack of assertiveness
- Poor organizational skills
- Imbalance between work and life
- Stagnation in comfort zones
- Insufficient feedback to direct reports

Wright

You've talked at length about one-on-one coaching. In today's business environment, so much work is performed in teams. What are the benefits of teamwork, and how can leaders build strong teams?

Wolf

Effective leaders understand that their organizations will realize substantial benefits by building strong teams to reach their objectives and strategic goals. Bringing people together on the same page is highly effective because people can accomplish more collectively than individually.

Every participant brings a unique skill set to the team. Some may be highly creative at coming up with new ideas, others may excel at details, and some have the ability to move the group's ideas forward and follow through to completion. It's very rare to find one person who has all of these skills. By working together and combining what everyone brings to the table, the group's goals will be realized so much faster.

Teamwork allows all participants to see the big picture, even though each member may be working on a limited component of a given project. Groups also make it very difficult for individuals to hide, and they enforce accountability. For example, if Mary doesn't complete her assignment on time and Jim doesn't do his job correctly, then James cannot do his job. Shared accountability distributes the workload fairly by splitting up a project and allowing different people to work on assigned tasks. The end result is rapid completion.

Teamwork also builds camaraderie and encourages open communication. When every member is focused on a single outcome, strong relationships and trust are built—one of the most important aspects of teamwork, if not the most important. Every team member must have complete trust in fellow participants as well as faith in others' desire to work in the best interests of the team and company.

When building a strong team, leaders must look at each member's strengths and abilities to determine whether the group can gel. When there's a good fit, teams will combine their strengths to achieve the group's overall goals. Leaders must also nurture team growth and development to ensure everyone contributes in a positive way.

To build strong teams, it's vital to develop a team culture that includes the following fundamentals:

- Defined expectations with clear goals, objectives, and a shared team vision
- An established timeline with individual and team accountability
- A clearly articulated purpose for the team's existence
- Team members' complete acknowledgment of the roles they play
- Well-defined processes and procedures on how the work will be accomplished
- Team access to all available resources required to reach the stated goal
- A diverse team composed of members with complementary skills
- Individual and group commitment to the work that will be performed
- The shared knowledge that each team member is valued and will be rewarded for hard work and effort
- Clear, honest, and open communication among all team members
- Rules of conduct, including steps to resolve any emerging conflicts

As companies struggle to grow and become more innovative, teams will become more important than ever before. Bringing together people with multiple skills and competencies leads to successful development of new products, services, and strategies.

Wright

There is so much talk these days about the multigenerational workplace, especially millennial workers. Can you describe their characteristics and outline effective ways to lead them?

Wolf

There are four different generations in today's workplace, David. The oldest is the Silent Generation—those born before 1945—who usually stay in the same job for long periods. They're loyal, hardworking team players who have developed excellent people skills such as listening, consensus-building, and teamwork.

Baby Boomers—those born between 1946 and 1964—are very competitive, ethical, and have strong values. Like the Silent Generation, they excel at developing relationships and building consensus. Unlike the Silent Generation, however, they usually hold several different jobs during their careers, which has allowed them to master a wide variety of experiences and accumulate an impressive degree of knowledge. Boomers' strong work ethic often causes them to put their jobs ahead of their families.

Generation Xers—those born between 1965 and 1980—are known for their skepticism. These workers saw their parents laid off from jobs as they were growing up. They were also the first generation to experience widespread divorce and family upheaval, so they truly value their work-life balance.

Millennials—those born after 1981—have been supervised and overindulged by their parents since the day they were born. They grew up using e-mail, text messaging, cell phones, video games, and the Internet, on which they heavily rely to find information and communicate. Because they're not used to having a lot of personal interaction, they lack social skills and appear to be rude. This group is just entering the workforce, and their ranks are growing so quickly that they may surpass the Baby Boomers in record time. Millennials want to work hard and move up the career ladder, but they tend to be impatient.

They don't want to wait too long for career advancement, and they'll change jobs frequently when they feel bored or unhappy.

Thanks to the Internet, Millennials are used to finding information quickly and they don't require long explanations of how to do something. They forge ahead and enjoy learning as they go, while older generations generally want more detailed explanations.

Millennials are used to structure and seek role models with whom they can build relationships. They want to be challenged and engage in as many learning opportunities as possible. They also have very high expectations and aren't interested in paying their dues. For this reason, leaders must coach, praise, and encourage them on a regular basis, as well as provide lots of positive feedback.

Millennials' enthusiasm should always be nurtured, and support should be readily available when they encounter more challenging situations. Leaders can accomplish this by allowing them to participate in teams with older workers, which has two enormous benefits: Millennials will improve their people skills, and more senior workers will become more proficient in modern technology. The older workers can offer advice on people and social skills, including teamwork, building relationships, and customer service. Partnering these groups facilitates growth among all generations.

Always keep in mind that Millennials want to work with similarly positive people within a friendly environment where everyone is treated with respect. They seek open, accessible leaders who demonstrate the utmost integrity. They'll never respect leaders based on age, longevity, and authority. What's most important to them is someone who shows them respect.

Wright

Work-life balance is an issue most business leaders face today, and you've cited it as one you often encounter when coaching leaders. With all of the pressure placed on leaders to execute and perform, what steps can they take to alleviate the problem?

Wolf

Leaders are working longer hours than ever before, making work-life balance a critical issue that won't go away soon. Certainly, technology has had a huge impact on our daily lives. Immediate access and availability through cell phones, BlackBerrys, and instant messaging, among other technologies, put a tremendous amount of pressure on leaders to respond quickly to both large and inconsequential problems.

When I coach executives who face this issue, some are unable to resolve it. They're literally tethered to their devices. As a result, they'll experience a loss of focus, lack of energy, and decline in decision-making ability, all of which may lead to job burnout, high stress levels, divorce, and even alcohol or drug dependency.

One of the most effective ways to combat work-life balance issues is through competent time management. When you efficiently manage your time, you'll have a more balanced life, a higher degree of productivity, less stress, and greater job satisfaction.

I often recommend several specific steps:

- Learn to say no. As leaders, we are always asked to take on more responsibilities, deadlines, and commitments. It's human nature to try to please everyone and expect more from ourselves, but we can easily accept more work than we're realistically capable of completing. Saying no in a professional way prevents you from overloading your schedule and accepting more than you can handle.
- Determine when you're at the peak of your day. People have peak and low periods during a workday. Determine when you're at your peak, and tackle the most important issues during this time.
- Create a not-to-do list composed of activities that need to be completed, but mustn't be personally handled by you.

Decide who you can empower to complete these tasks and delegate.

- Empower others. Surround yourself with great people and empower them with decision-making responsibilities.

- Establish a no-contact time. Close your office door for fifteen to thirty minutes each day. Let everyone know that you're not to be disturbed. Don't answer the phone or e-mails; instead, choose to work on issues that require your most immediate attention.

- Maintain your energy and be sure to exercise. Stay hydrated by drinking plenty of water and eat balanced meals. Go for five-minute walks two to three times a day.

- Implement periodic stand-up meetings. Much of what's accomplished in a one-hour meeting may well be handled in a fifteen- to thirty-minute gathering during which everyone stands. This keeps people on track and more focused, and important issues are resolved quickly.

Work-life balance involves more than time management. Leaders must recognize the need to slow down, enjoy life, and replenish their energy supply on a daily basis. Having a balanced life takes into account all your needs, which include family, friends, work, play, private time, exercise, and spiritual time. It is getting your priorities straight!

We often say we are working long hours for our families, but if we ask our families they will probably say they would like to have us around more. Take a moment out of your life and think about the impact you are making on each family member by working long hours. Then take a few minutes out of your busy day and try to figure out how to cut back and rearrange your priorities.

It takes discipline to do this and discipline is what leaders have. The key to achieving a balanced life is building it into your schedule like anything else and then making it a habit. Start today by making an action plan: Look at your schedule two to three weeks in advance and then block out time for the things you enjoy doing and the people you enjoy being with.

Making a commitment to work-life balance will make leaders more productive and better prepared to handle the daily grind of today's stressful business environment, while providing the time to enjoy the one life you will ever have.

Wright

Jeff, this has been a fascinating discussion, and I appreciate the time you've taken for this interview. I know our readers will find your suggestions very helpful in their quest to become better leaders. I am eager to read your upcoming book, *The Essence of Effective Leadership,* and I want to thank you for being with us on *Roadmap to Success.*

Wolf

Thank you, David. It has been a privilege to talk with you.

About the Author

Jeff Wolf, one of America's most dynamic speakers, is recognized as one of the top executive coaches in the country. A highly sought-after business consultant, his strategic focus in solving corporate and human issues has earned him continuing raves from national firms. He has been featured on NBC and FOX TV, and he's the author of the upcoming book, *The Essence of Effective Leadership.*

Jeff has worked with many of the largest corporations in the world. He served as CEO for one of the country's largest healthcare receivables-management companies and is the former CEO of a prestigious polling and political opinion research corporation. As a successful basketball coach, he was selected by Gillette as one of the country's outstanding coaches. He has appeared on national radio and television to promote leadership, teamwork, and positive attitudes.

Jeff is currently president of Wolf Management Consultants, one of the most comprehensive consulting, training, and coaching firms in the nation. The firm specializes in helping people, teams, and organizations achieve maximum effectiveness.

Throughout the years, he has been a recognized authority on leadership, and his principles, strategies, and inspiration have influenced dramatic growth and changes in countless organizations.

Jeff Wolf, President, RCC
Wolf Management Consultants, Inc.
Chicago Office: 5550 West Touhy Avenue, Suite 300
Skokie, Illinois 60077
Phone: 847-673-9090
Fax: 847-673-9850

San Diego Office: 2223 Avenida De La Playa, Suite 208
La Jolla, California 92037
Phone: 858-638-8260
Fax: 858-638-8229

jeff@wolfmotivation.com
www.wolfmotivation.com

An Interview with…

Dr. Kenneth Blanchard

Chapter Three

An interview with…

Dr. Kenneth Blanchard

David E. Wright (Wright)

Few people have created a positive impact on the day-to-day management of people and companies more than Dr. Kenneth Blanchard. He is known around the world simply as Ken, a prominent, gregarious, sought-after author, speaker, and business consultant. Ken is universally characterized by friends, colleagues, and clients as one of the most insightful, powerful, and compassionate men in business today. Ken's impact as a writer is far-reaching. His phenomenal best-selling book, *The One Minute Manager*®, coauthored with Spencer Johnson, has sold more than thirteen million copies worldwide and has been translated into more than twenty-five languages. Ken is Chairman and "Chief Spiritual Officer" of the Ken Blanchard Companies. The organization's focus is to energize organizations around the world with customized training in bottom-line business strategies based on the simple, yet powerful principles inspired by Ken's best-selling books.

Dr. Blanchard, welcome to *Roadmap to Success*.

Dr. Ken Blanchard (Blanchard)

Well, it's nice to talk with you, David. It's good to be here.

Wright

I must tell you that preparing for your interview took quite a bit more time than usual. The scope of your life's work and your business, the Ken Blanchard Companies, would make for a dozen fascinating interviews.

Before we dive into the specifics of some of your projects and strategies, will you give our readers a brief synopsis of your life—how you came to be the Ken Blanchard we all know and respect?

Blanchard

Well, I'll tell you, David, I think life is what you do when you are planning on doing something else. I think that was John Lennon's line. I never intended to do what I have been doing. In fact, all my professors in college told me that I couldn't write. I wanted to do college work, which I did, and they said, "You had better be an administrator." So I decided I was going to be a Dean of Students. I got provisionally accepted into my master's degree program and then provisionally accepted at Cornell because I never could take any of those standardized tests.

I took the college boards four times and finally got 502 in English. I don't have a test-taking mind. I ended up in a university in Athens, Ohio, in 1966 as an Administrative Assistant to the Dean of the Business School. When I got there he said, "Ken, I want you to teach a course. I want all my deans to teach." I had never thought about teaching because they said I couldn't write, and teachers had to publish. He put me in the manager's department.

I've taken enough bad courses in my day and I wasn't going to teach one. I really prepared and had a wonderful time with the students. I was chosen as one of the top ten teachers on the campus coming out of the chute!

I just had a marvelous time. A colleague by the name of Paul Hersey was chairman of the Management Department. He wasn't very friendly to me initially because the Dean had led me to his department, but I heard he was a great teacher. He taught Organizational Behavior and Leadership. So I said, "Can I sit in on your course next semester?"

"Nobody audits my courses," he said. "If you want to take it for credit, you're welcome."

I couldn't believe it. I had a doctoral degree and he wanted me to take his course for credit—so I signed up.

The registrar didn't know what to do with me because I already had a doctorate, but I wrote the papers and took the course, and it was great.

In June 1967, Hersey came into my office and said, "Ken, I've been teaching in this field for ten years. I think I'm better than anybody, but I can't write. I'm a nervous wreck, and I'd love to write a textbook with somebody. Would you write one with me?"

I said, "We ought to be a great team. You can't write and I'm not supposed to be able to, so let's do it!"

Thus began this great career of writing and teaching. We wrote a textbook called *Management of Organizational Behavior: Utilizing Human Resources.* It came out in its eighth edition October 3, 2000, and the ninth edition was published September 3, 2007. It has sold more than any other textbook in that area over the years. It's been over forty years since that book first came out.

I quit my administrative job, became a professor, and ended up working my way up the ranks. I got a sabbatical leave and went to California for one year twenty-five years ago. I ended up meeting Spencer Johnson at a cocktail party. He wrote children's books—a wonderful series called *Value Tales*® *for Kids.* He also wrote *The Value of Courage: The Story of Jackie Robinson* and *The Value of Believing In Yourself: The Story of Louis Pasteur.*

My wife, Margie, met him first and said, "You guys ought to write a children's book for managers because they won't read anything else." That was my introduction to Spencer. So, *The One Minute Manager* was really a kid's book for big people. That is a long way from saying that my career was well planned.

Wright

Ken, what and/or who were your early influences in the areas of business, leadership, and success? In other words, who shaped you in your early years?

Blanchard

My father had a great impact on me. He was retired as an admiral in the Navy and had a wonderful philosophy. I remember when I was elected as president of the seventh grade, and I came home all pumped up. My father said, "Son, it's great that you're the president of the seventh grade, but now that you have that leadership position, don't ever use it." He said, "Great leaders are followed because people respect them and like them, not because they have power." That was a wonderful lesson for me early on. He was just a great model for me. I got a lot from him.

Then I had this wonderful opportunity in the mid-1980s to write a book with Norman Vincent Peale. He wrote *The Power of Positive Thinking*. I met him when he was eighty-six years old; we were asked to write a book on ethics together, *The Power of Ethical Management: Integrity Pays, You Don't Have to Cheat to Win*. It didn't matter what we were writing together; I learned so much from him. He just built from the positive things I learned from my mother.

My mother said that when I was born I laughed before I cried, I danced before I walked, and I smiled before I frowned. So that, as well as Norman Vincent Peale, really impacted me as I focused on what I could do to train leaders. How do you make them positive? How do you make them realize that it's not about them, it's about who they are serving? It's not about their position—it's about what they can do to help other people win.

So, I'd say my mother and father, then Norman Vincent Peale. All had a tremendous impact on me.

Wright

I can imagine. I read a summary of your undergraduate and graduate degrees. I assumed you studied Business Administration, marketing management, and related courses. Instead, at Cornell you studied Government and Philosophy. You received your master's from Colgate in Sociology and Counseling and your PhD from Cornell in Educational Administration and Leadership. Why did you choose this course of study? How has it affected your writing and consulting?

Blanchard

Well, again, it wasn't really well planned out. I originally went to Colgate to get a master's degree in Education because I was going to be a Dean of Students over men. I had been a Government major, and I was a Government major because it was the best department at Cornell in the Liberal Arts School. It was exciting. We would study what the people were doing at the league of governments. And then, the Philosophy Department was great. I just loved the philosophical arguments. I wasn't a great student in terms of getting grades, but I'm a total learner. I would sit there and listen, and I would really soak it in.

When I went over to Colgate and got into the education courses, they were awful. They were boring. The second week, I was sitting at the bar at the Colgate Inn saying, "I can't believe I've been here two years for this." This is just the way the Lord works: Sitting next to me in the bar was a young sociology professor who had just gotten his PhD at Illinois. He was staying at the Inn. I was moaning and groaning about what I was doing, and he said, "Why don't you come and major with me in sociology? It's really exciting."

"I can do that?" I asked.

He said, "Yes."

I knew they would probably let me do whatever I wanted the first week. Suddenly, I switched out of Education and went with Warren Ramshaw. He had a tremendous impact on me. He retired some years ago as the leading professor at Colgate in the Arts and Sciences, and got me interested in leadership and organizations. That's why I got a master's in Sociology.

The reason I went into educational administration and leadership? It was a doctoral program I could get into because I knew the guy heading up the program. He said, "The greatest thing about Cornell is that you will be in the School of Education. It's not very big, so you don't have to take many education courses, and you can take stuff all over the place."

There was a marvelous man by the name of Don McCarty who eventually became the Dean of the School of Education, Wisconsin. He had an impact on my life; but I was always just searching around.

My mission statement is: to be a loving teacher and example of simple truths that help myself and others to awaken the presence of God in our lives. The reason I mention "God" is that I believe the biggest addiction in the world is the human ego; but I'm really into simple truth. I used to tell people I was trying to get the B.S. out of the behavioral sciences.

Wright

I can't help but think, when you mentioned your father, that he just bottom-lined it for you about leadership.

Blanchard

Yes.

Wright

A man named Paul Myers, in Texas, years and years ago when I went to a conference down there, said, "David, if you think you're a leader and you look around, and no one is following you, you're just out for a walk."

Blanchard

Well, you'd get a kick out of this—I'm just reaching over to pick up a picture of Paul Myers on my desk. He's a good friend, and he's a part of our Center for FaithWalk Leadership where we're trying to challenge and equip people to lead like Jesus. It's non-profit. I tell people I'm not an evangelist because we've got enough trouble with the Christians we have. We don't need any more new ones. But, this is a picture of Paul on top of a mountain. Then there's another picture below that of him under the sea with stingrays. It says, "Attitude is everything. Whether you're on the top of the mountain or the bottom of the sea, true happiness is achieved by accepting God's promises, and by having a biblically positive frame of mind. Your attitude is everything." Isn't that something?

Wright

He's a fine, fine man. He helped me tremendously. In keeping with the theme of our book, *Roadmap for Success,* I wanted to get a sense from you about your own success journey. Many people know you best from *The One Minute Manager* books you coauthored with Spencer Johnson. Would you consider these books as a high water mark for you or have you defined success for yourself in different terms?

Blanchard

Well, you know, *The One Minute Manager* was an absurdly successful book so quickly that I found I couldn't take credit for it. That was when I really got on my own spiritual journey and started to try to find out what the real meaning of life and success was.

That's been a wonderful journey for me because I think, David, the problem with most people is they think their self-worth is a function of their performance plus the opinion of others. The minute you think that is what your self-worth is, every day your self-worth is up for grabs because your performance is going to fluctuate on a day-to-day basis. People are fickle. Their opinions are going to go up and down. You need to ground your self-worth in the unconditional love that God has ready for us, and that really grew out of the unbelievable success of *The One Minute Manager.*

When I started to realize where all that came from, that's how I got involved in this ministry that I mentioned. Paul Myers is a part of it. As I started to read the Bible, I realized that everything I've ever written about, or taught, Jesus did. You know, He did it with the twelve incompetent guys He "hired." The only guy with much education was Judas, and he was His only turnover problem.

Wright

Right.

Blanchard

This is a really interesting thing. What I see in people is not only do they think their self-worth is a function of their performance plus the opinion of others, but they measure their success on the amount of accumulation of wealth, on recognition, power, and status. I think those are nice success items. There's nothing wrong with those, as long as you don't define your life by that.

What I think you need to focus on rather than success is what Bob Buford, in his book *Halftime,* calls "significance"—moving from success to significance. I think the opposite of accumulation of wealth is generosity.

I wrote a book called *The Generosity Factor* with Truett Cathy, who is the founder of Chick-fil-A. He is one of the most generous men I've ever met in my life. I thought we needed to have a model of generosity. It's not only your *treasure,* but it's your *time* and *talent.* Truett and I added *touch* as a fourth one.

The opposite of recognition is service. I think you become an adult when you realize you're here to serve rather than to be served.

Finally, the opposite of power and status is loving relationships. Take Mother Teresa as an example—she couldn't have cared less about recognition, power, and status because she was focused on generosity, service, and loving relationships; but she got all of that earthly stuff. If you focus on the earthly, such as money, recognition, and power, you're never going to get to significance. But if you focus on significance, you'll be amazed at how much success can come your way.

Wright

I spoke with Truett Cathy recently and was impressed by what a down-to-earth, good man he seems to be. When you start talking about him closing his restaurants on Sunday, all of my friends—when they found out I had talked to him—said, "Boy, he must be a great Christian man, but he's rich." I told them, "Well, to put his faith into perspective, by closing on Sunday it costs him $500 million a year."

He lives his faith, doesn't he?

Blanchard

Absolutely, but he still outsells everybody else.

Wright

That's right.

Blanchard

According to their January 25, 2007, press release, Chick-fil-A was the nation's second-largest quick-service chicken restaurant chain in sales at that time. Its business performance marks the thirty-ninth consecutive year the chain has enjoyed a system-wide sales gain—a streak the company has sustained since opening its first chain restaurant in 1967.

Wright

The simplest market scheme, I told him, tripped me up. I walked by his first Chick-fil-A I had ever seen, and some girl came out with chicken stuck on toothpicks and handed me one; I just grabbed it and ate it; it's history from there on.

Blanchard

Yes, I think so. It's really special. It is so important that people understand generosity, service, and loving relationships because too many people are running around like a bunch of peacocks. You even see pastors who measure their success by how many are in their congregation; authors by how many books they have sold; businesspeople by what their profit margin is—how good sales are. The reality is, that's all well and good, but I think what you need to focus on is the other. I think if business did that more and we got Wall Street off our backs with all the short-term evaluation, we'd be a lot better off.

Wright

Absolutely. There seems to be a clear theme that winds through many of your books that has to do with success in business and organizations—how people are treated by management and how they feel about their value to a company. Is this an accurate observation? If so, can you elaborate on it?

Blanchard

Yes, it's a very accurate observation. See, I think the profit is the applause you get for taking care of your customers and creating a motivating environment for your people. Very often people think that business is only about the bottom line. But no, that happens to be the result of creating raving fan customers, which I've described with Sheldon Bowles in our book, *Raving Fans*. Customers want to brag about you, if you create an environment where people can be gung-ho and committed. You've got to take care of your customers and your people, and then your cash register is going to go ka-ching, and you can make some big bucks.

Wright

I noticed that your professional title with the Ken Blanchard Companies is somewhat unique—"Chairman and Chief Spiritual Officer." What does your title mean to you personally and to your company? How does it affect the books you choose to write?

Blanchard

I remember having lunch with Max DuPree one time. The legendary Chairman of Herman Miller, Max wrote a wonderful book called *Leadership Is an Art.*

"What's your job?" I asked him.

He said, "I basically work in the vision area."

"Well, what do you do?" I asked.

"I'm like a third-grade teacher," he replied. "I say our vision and values over, and over, and over again until people get it right, right, right."

I decided from that, I was going to become the Chief Spiritual Officer, which means I would be working in the vision, values, and energy part of our business. I ended up leaving a morning message every day for everybody in our company. We have twenty-eight international offices around the world.

I leave a voice mail every morning, and I do three things on that as Chief Spiritual Officer: One, people tell me who we need to pray for. Two, people tell me who we need to praise—our unsung heroes and people like that. And then three, I leave an inspirational morning message. I really am the cheerleader—the Energizer Bunny—in our company. I'm the reminder of why we're here and what we're trying to do.

We think that our business in the Ken Blanchard Companies is to help people lead at a higher level, and to help individuals and organizations. Our mission statement is to unleash the power and potential of people and organizations for the common good. So if we are going to do that, we've really got to believe in that.

I'm working on getting more Chief Spiritual Officers around the country. I think it's a great title and we should get more of them.

Wright

So those people for whom you pray, where do you get the names?

Blanchard

The people in the company tell me who needs help, whether it's a spouse who is sick or kids who are sick or if they are worried about something. We've got over five years of data about the power of prayer, which is pretty important.

One morning, my inspirational message was about my wife and five members of our company who walked sixty miles one weekend—twenty miles a day for three days—to raise money for breast cancer research.

It was amazing. I went down and waved them all in as they came. They had a ceremony; they had raised $7.6 million. There were over three thousand people walking. A lot of the walkers were dressed in pink—they were cancer victors—people who had overcome it. There were even men walking with pictures of their wives who had died from breast cancer. I thought it was incredible.

There wasn't one mention about it in the major San Diego papers. I said, "Isn't that just something." We have to be an island of positive influence because all you see in the paper today is about celebrities and their bad behavior. Here you have all these thousands of people out there walking and trying to make a difference, and nobody thinks it's news.

So every morning I pump people up about what life's about, about what's going on. That's what my Chief Spiritual Officer job is about.

Wright

I had the pleasure of reading one of your releases, *The Leadership Pill*.

Blanchard

Yes.

Wright

I must admit that my first thought was how short the book was. I wondered if I was going to get my money's worth, which by the way, I most certainly did. Many of your books are brief and based on a fictitious story. Most business books in the market today are hundreds of pages in length and are read almost like a textbook.

Will you talk a little bit about why you write these short books, and about the premise of *The Leadership Pill?*

Blanchard

I really developed my relationship with Spencer Johnson when we wrote *The One Minute Manager.* As you know, he wrote, *Who Moved My Cheese,* which was a phenomenal success. He wrote children's books and is quite a storyteller.

Jesus taught by parables, which were short stories.

My favorite books are *Jonathan Livingston Seagull* and *The Little Prince.* Og Mandino, author of seventeen books, was the greatest of them all.

I started writing parables because people can get into the story and learn the contents of the story, and they don't bring their judgmental hats into reading. You write a regular book and they'll say, "Well, where did you get the research?" They get into that judgmental side. Our books get them emotionally involved and they learn.

The Leadership Pill is a fun story about a pharmaceutical company that thinks they have discovered the secret to leadership, and they can put the ingredients in a pill. When they announce it, the country goes crazy because everybody knows we need more effective leaders. When they release it, it outsells Viagra.

The founders of the company start selling off stock and they call them Pillionaires. But along comes this guy who calls himself "the effective manager," and he challenges them to a no-pill challenge. If they identify two non-performing groups, he'll take on one and let somebody on the pill take another one, and he guarantees he will outperform that person by the end of the year. They agree, but of course they give him a drug test every week to make sure he's not sneaking pills on the side.

I wrote the book with Marc Muchnick, who is a young guy in his early thirties. We did a major study of what this interesting "Y" generation—the young people of today—want from leaders, and this is a secret blend that this effective manager uses. When you think about it, David, it is really powerful in terms of what people want from a leader.

Number one, they want integrity. A lot of people have talked about that in the past, but these young people will walk if they see people say one thing and do another. A lot of us walk to the bathroom and out into the halls to talk about it. But these people will quit. They don't want somebody to say something and not do it.

The second thing they want is a partnership relationship. They hate superior/subordinate. I mean, what awful terms those are. You know, the "head" of the department and the hired "hands"—you don't even give them a head. "What do I do? I'm in supervision. I see things a lot clearer than these stupid idiots." They want to be treated as partners; if they can get a financial partnership, great. If they can't, they really want a minimum of a psychological partnership where they can bring their brains to work and make decisions.

Then finally, they want affirmation. They not only want to be caught doing things right, but they want to be affirmed for who they are. They want to be known as individual people, not as numbers.

So those are the three ingredients that this effective manager uses. They are wonderful values when you think about them.

Rank-order values for any organization is number one, integrity. In our company we call it ethics. It is our number one value. The number two value is partnership. In our company we call it relationships. Number three is affirmation—being affirmed as a human being. I think that ties into relationships, too. They are wonderful values that can drive behavior in a great way.

Wright

I believe most people in today's business culture would agree that success in business has everything to do with successful leadership. In *The Leadership Pill*, you present a simple but profound premise; that leadership is not something you do to people; it's something you do *with* them. At face value, that seems incredibly obvious. But you must have found in your research and observations that leaders in today's culture do not get this. Would you speak to that issue?

Blanchard

Yes. I think what often happens in this is the human ego. There are too many leaders out there who are self-serving. They're not leaders who have service in mind. They think the sheep are there for the benefit of the shepherd. All the power, money, fame, and recognition move up the hierarchy. They forget that the real action in business is not up the hierarchy—it's in the one-to-one, moment-to-moment interactions that your frontline people have with your customers. It's how the phone is answered. It's how problems are dealt with and those kinds of things. If you don't think that you're doing leadership *with* them—rather, you're doing it *to* them—after a while they won't take care of your customers.

I was at a store once (not Nordstrom's, where I normally would go) and I thought of something I had to share with my wife, Margie. I asked the guy behind the counter in Men's Wear, "May I use your phone?"

He said, "No!"

"You're kidding me," I said. "I can always use the phone at Nordstrom's."

"Look, buddy," he said, "they won't let *me* use the phone here. Why should I let you use the phone?"

That is an example of leadership that's done *to* employees, not *with* them. People want a partnership. People want to be involved in a way that really makes a difference.

Wright

Dr. Blanchard, the time has flown by and there are so many more questions I'd like to ask you. In closing, would you mind sharing with our readers some thoughts on success? If you were mentoring a small group of men and women, and one of their central goals was to become successful, what kind of advice would you give them?

Blanchard

Well, I would first of all say, "What are you focused on?" If you are focused on success as being, as I said earlier, accumulation of money, recognition, power, or status, I think you've got the wrong target. What you need to really be focused on is how you can be generous in the use of your time and your talent and your treasure and touch. How can you serve people rather than be served? How can you develop caring, loving relationships with people? My sense is if you will focus on those things, success in the traditional sense will come to you. But if you go out and say, "Man, I'm going to make a fortune, and I'm going to do this," and have that kind of attitude, you might get some of those numbers. I think you become an adult, however, when you realize you are here to give rather than to get. You're here to serve, not to be served. I would just say to people, "Life is such a very special occasion. Don't miss it by aiming at a target that bypasses other people, because we're really here to serve each other."

Wright

Well, what an enlightening conversation, Dr. Blanchard. I really want you to know how much I appreciate all the time you've taken with me for this interview. I know that our readers will learn from this, and I really appreciate your being with us today.

Blanchard

Well, thank you so much, David. I really enjoyed my time with you. You've asked some great questions that made me think, and I hope my answers are helpful to other people because as I say, life is a special occasion.

Wright

Today we have been talking with Dr. Ken Blanchard. He is coauthor of the phenomenal best-selling book, *The One Minute Manager*. The fact that he's the Chief Spiritual Officer of his company should make us all think about how we are leading our companies and leading our families and leading anything, whether it is in church or civic organizations. I know I will.

Thank you so much, Dr. Blanchard, for being with us today.

Blanchard

Good to be with you, David.

About the Author

Few people have created more of a positive impact on the day-to-day management of people and companies than Dr. Kenneth Blanchard, who is known around the world simply as "Ken."

When Ken speaks, he speaks from the heart with warmth and humor. His unique gift is to speak to an audience and communicate with each individual as if they were alone and talking one-on-one. He is a polished storyteller with a knack for making the seemingly complex easy to understand.

Ken has been a guest on a number of national television programs, including *Good Morning America* and *The Today Show*. He has been featured in *Time, People, U.S. News & World Report*, and a host of other popular publications.

He earned his bachelor's degree in Government and Philosophy from Cornell University, his master's degree in Sociology and Counseling from Colgate University, and his PhD in Educational Administration and Leadership from Cornell University.

Dr. Ken Blanchard
The Ken Blanchard Companies
125 State Place
Escondido, California 92029
800.728.6000
Fax: 760.489.8407
www.kenblanchard.com

Notes